A Day Never Ends if a Memory is Made

A Day Never Ends if a Memory is Made

ROSS ROBERTS

StoryTerrace

Text Martin Milnes, on behalf of StoryTerrace
Copyright © Ross Roberts and StoryTerrace
Text is private and confidential

First print November 2023

www.StoryTerrace.com

CONTENTS

THE SHOW'

INTRODUCTION:'... ALL I NEED IS AN HOUR OR TWO,TO TELL THE TALE OF A DREAMER LIKE YOU.'

Sometimes, in my deepest thought processes, I often overanalyse. I think to myself, *Am I doing the right thing? Am I in the right place? Is this the plan for my life?* And every now and again, the universe will say, 'Hey, Ross! Yes, you are! And yes, it is!'

I've been told that my spirit guide is an Indian chief, and he has a stick. Every time he wants me to realise I'm where I need to be, it's like he's hitting me over the head, with stars and glitter coming out of the stick. That's how I imagine it, anyway.

Turning 40 has allowed me to think back. More than ever, I'm grateful for my memories. I've always said, *'A day never ends if a memory is made.'* Thanks to Seabourn, my memories never fail to astound me. Sarah Brightman sang 'Happy Birthday' to me in the Thomas Keller Restaurant. In Ephesus, I addressed our guests from the stage of an ancient amphitheatre. West End star Ruthie Henshall dedicated 'Broadway Baby' to me.

But, dear reader and valued guest, I hope you might enjoy sharing in my *other* memories. The ones which made me Ross. Memories created with incredible people who shaped my life. Like all good shows, these memories encompass rise and fall, highs and lows, laughter and tears.

But above all, to quote Sir Tim Rice from *Joseph and the Amazing Technicolor Dreamcoat*, these memories encompass …

'… *the story of a boy whose dreams came true.*'

And he dedicates this book to Mum.

Author's Note:
All chapter titles are lyrics by Sir Tim Rice from
'Joseph And The Amazing Technicolor Dreamcoat'

1. 'MAY I RETURN TO THE BEGINNING ...'

My parents – Richard Alan Roberts and Jean Rebecca Haynes – met in 1974 through one of Mum's close friends. Her name was Shirley, and she was rather interested in Dad's brother, John. One night, she dragged Mum along for a night out with the brothers at The Coronation Club in Old Dalby, Leicestershire.

When Dad first saw Mum, as he didn't really know what to say, he decided to order food from the bar. Chicken and chips. His first words to Mum were, 'Do you want to a bit of chicken?' They began courting despite the distance between Mum's Nottinghamshire village of Tithby and Dad's base at RAF Lyneham in Wiltshire.

Dad, for whom Old Dalby was home, was an RAF ground engineer. He began as a Leading Aircraftsman (LAC) before promotion to Senior Aircraftsman (SAC) and Junior Technician (JT). Then, he rose to Corporal and finally Sergeant. Dad had always wanted to be a pilot, but sadly, his eyesight wasn't good enough.

On 24th March 1978, Richard and Jean became Mr. and Mrs Roberts. They married in the church next to Mum's childhood home, where my grandma still lives. For generations, this tiny, tiny church has been part of every major event in our family's lives. Christenings, marriages, and funerals have all taken place there.

At the wedding, Dad wore his Forces uniform; Mum dazzled in a gorgeous lace gown. To whisk the bride to the ceremony, they'd hired a beautiful black car with a yellow carriage … but the distance from Mum's house to the church was less than five metres! Mum, however, had a great idea, announcing to the driver, 'We'll just go around the block once and then pull up outside the church.' Well, on that drive, everything which *could* have gone wrong *did!* Farmers took sheep across the road. There were cows in the way … so, of course, she arrived late.

In the days leading up to the ceremony, Mum had warned Dad, 'Don't you dare drink the night before! If I smell it on you, I'll be furious!' But when Mum reached the altar, all through the vows, she sniffed the stench of whiskey. She began poking Dad, whispering through gritted teeth.

'You promised me you wouldn't drink last night!'

'But I haven't!' he hissed back. 'I didn't even go out! I went to bed early!' Now Mum was kicking him, growling, 'I can smell it on you!'

But it turned out that Dad was completely innocent. It was the vicar who'd been drinking! And just to top it all off, it rained on their wedding day. Ever after, on their anniversaries, they jokingly said, 'It rained at our wedding, and it's rained ever since!'

Soon after, Dad was reposted. They lived on the base camp at RAF Coningsby, Lincolnshire, where my brother Karl was born on 22nd December 1980. I then came along on 21st August 1983, born in the Lincolnshire town of Boston. Not long after, Dad was posted abroad to RAF Laarbruch, literally on the border between Germany and Holland. When armed guards raised the barrier to leave the camp, you'd drive a tiny distance to another barrier, and *that* was the border to Holland.

My earliest memories are from our flat on the base, home for the next six years. Karl and I shared a room with two single beds, although at first, I had a cot. As soon as I was old enough, I wanted to climb out and cuddle with Karl, which I often managed.

Our beds were separated by a chest of drawers, on which we kept a bright yellow ghetto blaster with double cassettes and a long radio aerial. Well! Did *we* think we were the hottest kids in town having *that* in our room?! In the lounge, we had a huge music system with a microphone for recording. We felt cock of the walk with that, too!

I have fond memories of Germany. We often visited a theme park inspired by the Brothers Grimm's fairy tales. Trash cans sang at you when rubbish was thrown in, so Karl and I constantly ran about gathering litter. At Christmas, we had advent calendars with little toys behind each door (very unusual at the time). They were kept in Mum and Dad's bedroom, so we'd dash in every morning, so excited.

Lorna Jane, who lived directly opposite, was my first-ever female friend, and she always went to ballet class. I wanted to go with her, and eventually, my parents let me. I don't remember much about the dancing, but I do remember the music and fun we had. All the children at the camp were around our age, so there were often joint birthday parties in our communal garden, with three-legged and egg-and-spoon races. The dads came together and built a Wendy House in that garden, too, with big painted cartoon characters.

As a family, we took weekend drives past Holland's fields of tulips. Whenever Karl and I saw a windmill, we'd burst into song: 'A Windmill In Old Amsterdam.'

> *'I saw a mouse!*
> *(Where?)*
> *There on the stair!*
> *(Where on the stair?)*
> *Right there!*
> *A little mouse with clogs on …'*

Mum used to love this because it really annoyed Dad!

Around the age of five, Karl and I began putting on little performances in our living room. This was mostly for Christmas or birthdays when our grandparents flew over. Our most memorable show was 'When Santa Got Stuck Up The Chimney.' Mum had a two-and-half-foot woven laundry basket, which I hid inside with the lid on, pretending it was the chimney. Meanwhile, Karl stood next to it and sang the first line, *'When Santa got stuck up the chimney, he began to shout …'*. On his last word, I'd burst out, wriggling, dressed as Santa, and in a deep, funny voice declared, *'You girls and boys won't get any toys if you don't pull me out!'* I remember this well because, by now, I felt my love for performing and anything artistic stirring inside me.

During my earliest years, I had an extremely bad stutter, but whenever I sang, it disappeared. The first time I spoke without difficulty was on my sixth birthday. At my party, I turned to Lorna Jane and asked, 'Could you pass me the crisps, please?' Mum looked astounded and gasped, 'What did you say?' Oblivious, I just replied, 'I asked Lorna to pass me the crisps.' 'But you didn't stutter!' Mum cried. From that day on, it just completely vanished – very bizarre.

Karl enjoyed singing, too, but was much more inspired than me by Dad's engineering job. Surrounded on the base by machinery, grease, and oil smells, Karl enjoyed making plastic Airfix models. One was particularly big, and he'd spent forever glueing and painting it. As we played outside, Mum appeared on the balcony, holding the model. We lived on the highest level, three floors up, and she shouted down, 'Karl, your plane looks amazing! Does it actually fly?' And with that, she threw the plane over the balcony, genuinely believing it would. I remember it all happening as if in slow motion, the plane crashing to the ground. Mum never forgave herself for that and felt absolutely terrible!

Karl and I attended Mass First School on the base camp. The uniform was a white shirt with a little green tie. There was a huge oak tree in the courtyard, surrounded by paving slabs. Other children played 'Chase' around that tree, but I never joined in as Karl had tripped and smashed his teeth on the slabs.

When I was six, we moved back to England. I don't remember much about it other than being excited to live closer to family. Dad was posted to RAF West Raynham in Norfolk. Again, Karl and I went to school on the base … but this wasn't a great time for us. We were bullied relentlessly. It was so bad that Mum got a job as a playground monitor just so she could be there for us.

With an August birthday, I was the youngest and smallest in my year group, which the bullies relished. They called me thick and dumb. When I was six, I had classmates who were eight, and at that age, there was a big difference in developmental skills. The UK curriculum was far more advanced than Germany's, so in maths and reading, I never understood what was being asked of me. We had a sandpit in the classroom, raised up on legs, and I often sat beneath it by myself.

Karl, meanwhile, was bullied because of his thick NHS glasses, big bushy hair, and chipped teeth. Neither of us made friends because, by that time, the other kids, having only ever known this school, had formed their friendship groups. Our escape was Saturday trips to Hunstanton, walking along the beaches, playing in arcades, and eating fish and chips.

I don't remember much else about Norfolk except for one thing. After a really rough school week, Mum and Dad wanted to cheer me up. My great passion was music, and I was a massive fan of Kylie Minogue. So, Mum and Dad went to Woolworths and bought me, on cassette tape, Kylie's debut studio album. It was called *Kylie* – the one with the angled hat and wavy hair on the cover. They'd also bought me Jason Donovan's debut album, *Ten Good Reasons,* with the white shirt and red background. Back then, cassettes weren't cheap. As a kid, I never wanted stuff, but at the same time, we weren't affluent. So, receiving these albums, I felt like the most amazing child in the world, playing them constantly.

However, as we'd been so unhappy, Mum and Dad decided we should live off-base. Dad requested a transfer to RAF Cottesmore, so they began searching for places back in Nottinghamshire. In 1989, my parents made an offer on a house in Cramner Avenue, Whatton, where we moved that November. It remains my house to this day.

Karl and I attended Archbishop Cramner School (the namesake of our road, honouring the Nottinghamshire-born Archbishop of Canterbury during Henry VIII's reign). This was a much happier school experience, which I really enjoyed, surrounded by fields with a little orchard next to the playground.

It was here that I got back into singing. At the end of each academic year, there was an awards ceremony. Beforehand, there was always some kind of performance, like a choir, a dance routine, or a gymnastics display. One year, we did a show with music inspired by *Cats*.... only it was called *Rats*, based on the story of the Pied Piper. It was absolutely horrific!

If there wasn't a big performance planned, I was very often asked to sing a solo. One year, I decided on 'Any Dream Will Do' from Andrew Lloyd Webber and Tim Rice's *Joseph and the Amazing Technicolor Dreamcoat*. I wound the cassette tape to the correct place, ready to sing along with the cast album. As the teacher went to press 'play', there was a hustle and bustle of kids muttering, 'Oh, he's gonna sing'. But then the wrong music came on. I heard, *'Some folks dream of the wonders they'll do ...'* It was the opening song of the show; someone had wound the cassette right back to the very beginning! So, I turned around, slightly diva-like, and

19

announced, 'It's at the wrong point! That's the wrong song.' I learned a valuable lesson that day: always check and double-check your tracks and cues!

The following year, it was announced that *Joseph* would be our school production. People kept asking if I was going to play the title role, to which I answered, 'Well, I don't know.' Although it was a coy reply, secretly, of course, I desperately wanted that part. Like Charlie dreaming of a Golden Ticket to the chocolate factory, Joseph was like my own Golden Ticket!

Then, in preparation for auditions, the school organised a trip to see *Joseph* in the West End at the London Palladium. Visiting London was a major event, and a payment plan was devised for the parents; kids brought in £5 a week until everything was paid off. Off we went to see a Wednesday matinee, the coach driver showing us London sites en route: Buckingham Palace Nelson's Column. Travelling from a town in the middle of nowhere to this metropolis of iconic scenery was awe-inspiring. My love for London began that day. Even now, going to London feels like a special treat.

As we queued outside the Palladium, I gazed at the *Joseph* posters in their big brass frames. For some reason, they all showed Jason Donovan, even though by now, he'd left and been replaced by Phillip Schofield. My lasting memory is the big finale reprise of 'Any Dream Will Do': '*Give me my coloured coat, my amazing coloured coat …*' Phillip Schofield stood on a platform lifted out into the auditorium. His coat expanded until the coloured material stretched the entire width of the house. My heart raced. My emotions soared.

Dazzled, with goose pimples on my arms, this was a life-defining moment.

At this performance, the theatre was packed with school kids, so afterwards, there was a Q&A with one of the actors. I vividly remember him being a Swing – an ensemble member who understudied multiple parts (and could be thrown on stage at a moment's notice if someone had an injury mid-show).

This guy walked out wearing a trendy bomber jacket and sat on the edge of the stage with one knee up, chatting about his daily life. I was too awestruck to ask anything ... but I vividly remember thinking, *Hang on! This guy gets to perform on stage, singing and dancing, living in London, doing this amazing show eight times a week ... and that's his job?!* This blew my little mind! I'd never been to the theatre before, so it had never occurred to me that people could do this professionally.

Now, I knew what I wanted to do in life. I wanted to be on stage. I wanted to be in front of an audience. I don't think I slept a wink that night; my adrenaline was through the roof. As a result, to this day, *Joseph* remains one of my all-time favourite musicals.

Next, of course, we had auditions. Sadly, I didn't get the role of Joseph. Our school was quite progressive for the early '90s ... the part went to a girl! Her name was Natasha Marquess, and I must say, she was fantastic. Of course, I was upset at first but quickly accepted that it wasn't my time to shine. Just because I was the only schoolboy who sang, it didn't mean that I'd automatically get the main parts.

However, this moment set a trend throughout my life ... to this day, I have never been cast in the lead role in any production I've ever done. On this occasion, I was given the chorus part of a 'Hairy Ishmaelite'. I took my role very seriously, wearing my homemade colourful cardboard hat (saying 'Ishmaelite') and the most vividly bright T-shirt (almost neon) you could imagine!

My big moment, however, came not long after ... by accident. I was taking part in the annual 'Gang Show'. This was a huge event performed at Nottingham's Theatre Royal by local Scouts, Cubs, Brownies, and Girl Guides. There was a big production number – 'The Old Bazaar in Cairo' – and I was cast as a belly dancer in a silk purple outfit. After each person sang their solo line, they ran up to the back while the next group ran down for their moment.

However, running was quite difficult on a raked stage (meaning that the stage slopes downwards). One night, I slipped ... and I mean *properly* slipped. This wasn't just a little oopsie-slip. This was a proper slapstick *Home Alone* slip, landing with my legs high in the air! Then, I began to slide down towards the audience. I vividly remember the entire house roaring with laughter. After getting back up, with a flick of my head scarf and dramatic adjustment to my bikini top, I made it clear that the show must go on.

This, however, was another 'Eureka' moment. *Oh!* I thought to myself. *I enjoyed the thrill of getting that audience reaction.* Of course, I'd had fun performing as part of a group, but I liked even *more* that *I'd* done something to make a packed theatre of complete strangers laugh. This was no longer just my family in the living room! It was a real thrill to realise the power and impact of comedy.

Back at school that same year, it was time for the end-of-year presentation ceremony. For years, there had never been any kind of creative award, so twelve months previously, Mrs Lomax, who ran the choir, had founded The Shirley Lomax Cup For Singing. The first recipient, in his leaving year, had been my brother Karl. This year, everyone assumed that Natasha would win because she'd played Joseph (and she was leaving).

As there was no major performance prior to the ceremony, once again, I was asked to sing. For some reason, Mrs Lomax had specifically chosen a song called 'Picking Teams'.

When we pick teams in the playground
Whatever the game might be
There's always somebody left till last
And usually it's me …

It was so sad! The last section went …

Maybe if teams were sometimes picked
Starting with the worst,
Once in his life a boy like me
Could end up being first!

Once I'd finished singing, Mr Twells, the Headmaster, walked over and announced, 'Well, I'm sure that's not true, Ross. But there's something I have here for you. And it's not being picked for the team. It's the Shirley Lomax Cup For Singing!'

I genuinely hadn't even considered I might win – I wasn't even leaving! But now my name would be engraved right there beneath Karl's. It was a total surprise, and I felt extremely proud. Mum and Grandma were in the audience; Mum celebrated so loudly that I think she enjoyed the moment even more than me!

One particular mother at school was a real busybody. Her kids, as expected, had won several sports awards, but now she came over to Mum and gushed, 'Oh, you must be so proud!'. Mum had quite strong opinions about this woman, so she definitely wasn't going to let this triumph pass … she was going to make the most of it!

'Well!' she faux-modestly smiled, 'It's come as a bit of a surprise, actually. I'm going to have a clear-out to ensure it takes pride of place on the mantelpiece. Two years in a row for the Roberts family!'

Richard Alan Roberts, my dad in his early RAF days

Mum and Dad at the first official family event as a couple

Gang Show, the belly dancers singing 'The Old Bizarre in Cairo' me in Purple silk

24th March 1978 time to get married

Mum in her handmade lace gown, looking stunning

My first photograph, in my incubator, with a glowing mum, and proud brother Karl.

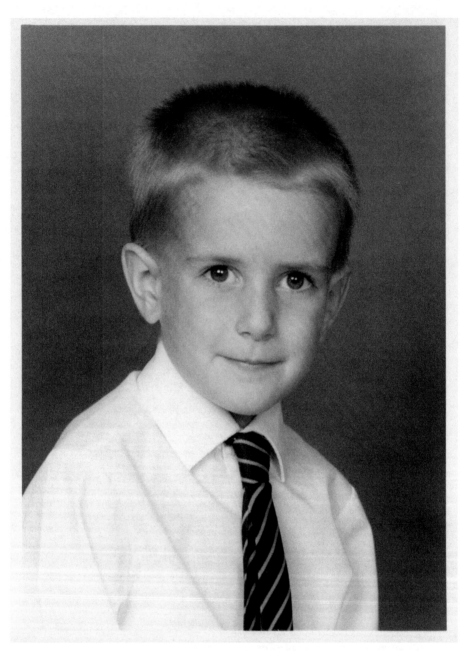

Young Ross aged 5 at Mass First School in Germany

My Santa outfit from our little 'When Santa got stuck up the chimney' performance

Dads proud of their playhouse creation

Christmas Eve 1989, Christmas in our new family home in Nottingham

2. 'LET US GRAB HIM NOW, DO HIM IN WHILE WE'VE GOT THE TIME'

The secondary school was Toot Hill Comprehensive in Bingham. Moving here wasn't too intimidating as I knew Karl's Year Nine friends, who'd been over to our house. They were part of the school choir, which I joined as soon as I arrived. I sat with these Year Nine kids for lunch before running to rehearsals, so I was always around slightly older people.

School productions were usually plays, but during my first year, Toot Hill produced an original musical, *The Devil You Know*, by a local writer. It was about William Booth, the Nottingham-born founder of the Salvation Army. Naturally, the lead roles went to older kids, but I had one line after a woman got knocked down by a vegetable cart. I ran over dramatically and cried, 'She's certainly skin and bone, poor thing!'. It may have been just one line, but I milked it flamboyantly.

Around this time, I joined a Saturday drama school in the neighbouring town of Radcliffe. It was called 11th Session, and I really enjoyed my acting classes with the brilliantly supportive Mrs. Wyles (who, coincidentally, was also my school form tutor). As Nottingham was home to Central Studios, I attended open auditions and workshops for TV. I didn't get any screen work but dedicated all my spare time to performing, including as 'Friedrich' in Bingham Amateur Operatic Society's production of *The Sound of Music.*

During rehearsals, I became great friends with Daniel, the boy playing 'Kurt'. I was obsessed with the Spice Girls, so when Daniel bought me their latest singles, I was so happy and very touched. Back then, buying music involved real effort; Daniel had been all the way to HMV in Nottingham just for me.

Later, I played 'Enoch Snow Jr' in *Carousel.* Mum and Dad came to all my shows, but Dad wasn't a fan of this one. It ended with 'You'll Never Walk Alone', and as a lifelong supporter of Nottingham Forest, he wasn't keen on me singing the Liverpool FC anthem!

A few years later, it was time for the next school production. As *The Devil You Know* had made Toot Hill far more money than any play, they decided on another big musical: *Jesus Christ Superstar.* As noted, there was a casting hierarchy, with older kids getting their pick of principal roles. By this time, however, the main two older 'Theatre Boys' had left. As I was now in Year Ten, I believed, I hoped, I dreamed this would be my chance. Surely, I'd be in line to play Jesus …

But then a new kid came along from Year Nine- Frazer Warriner. I'll never forget him (and Dad remembers his name to this day). Frazer was given Jesus. I was devastated! Yet again, I was fated not to be the leading man. Instead, I was cast as King Herod. Looking back, though, I totally see this was the right part for me. Herod is a wonderful character role;

34

he might only have one number, but it *is* the best song in the show.

I made my entrance on a trolley pushed by a harem of girls in black cocktail dresses. As I sang, another eight girls danced in top hats and sparkly shirts while my harem posed on the stairs. They were instructed to give 'come hither' looks to boys in the audience. Any girl that fancied it was allowed to push my trolley. Loads of girls began fighting to do it but not to be close to me. They just wanted to flutter their lashes at the school heartthrob watching that night!

For a school production, I still think our *Jesus Christ Superstar* was pretty good. But afterwards, I felt that empty nothingness which often hits actors when their shows close. You've been on a high for months with auditions, rehearsals, and performances…then suddenly, it ends, and you feel like you don't have any purpose. A void is left; you descend back to reality after the applause fades.

To lift my spirits, I was forever upstairs in my bedroom, stomping around, singing and dancing. The first ever single I'd bought (at HMV for 49p) was 'Trouble' by a girl group named Shampoo. Walking around music shops gave me such a buzz, and I'd even take my Walkman everywhere to listen as soon as I left the store! As noted, the Spice Girls were my ultimate favourites. In fact, whenever I had enough money, I always bought two copies of each single to help them reach the top of the charts! Getting to see their music videos, however, was challenging as we didn't have cable TV. Fortunately, help was at hand.

I had a friend at school named Paul, but he was way more popular than me, with a lot more street cred, so we were only friends because our mums were friends! Paul had cable TV and recorded the Spice Girls' music videos for me onto VHS tapes. He'd hand them over at school but in secret. No one was allowed to know that we were friends. He didn't want to be seen in public with someone of a different social status!

At home, I'd use Paul's videos to learn the Spice Girls' dances and go to extreme lengths to get them right. We had a full-length mirror on the wall of our landing. I'd open my bedroom door and place my TV-video-combi on the floor. Then, I'd watch the dance routines in the mirror. That way, I'd be doing the exact same moves (as if I were on stage) and not copying everything the wrong way around (as if watching from the audience). From now on, at any party, if they played a Spice Girls song – or any hit by any pop star – I knew every move, every lyric, and even every breath the artists took.

The local Nottingham radio station was 96 Trent FM, on which presenter Simon Dale hosted music trivia competitions. Often, the prizes were albums released just that week – perhaps Christina Aguilera, B*Witched or a movie soundtrack. Sometimes, it was cinema tickets. Other times, big prize giveaways had autographed items. For three years, I entered each competition and somehow always won. The DJs knew me by name. But when the prize was 'Win Your Height In CDs', I picked them up from the radio station to find I'd been short-changed! Plus, it was all folk, rap and heavy metal. Not quite the Britney, Madonna and Destiny's Child haul of music I'd hoped!

In my later years at school, I did more stage productions. I loved our Sixth Form pantos, cheap and no-frills as they were. These were written, performed, produced, directed, and designed entirely by us pupils. In *Aladdin,* I played Jafaar's assistant, Ronson. The character had been written for me and was described as a 'camp sidekick'. I wore a black T-shirt with the word 'Fruity' written in sequins! I had an absolute ball, ad-libbing all over the place.

Those pantos really brought everyone together, but perhaps I'm looking back through rose-tinted specs. You see, with regard to secondary school, this wasn't the full story ...

The bullying began in year seven. Never physical. Just mental. Mostly name-calling. People had labelled me 'gay' ever since primary school. Back then, I didn't know what 'gay' was. So, it had been ingrained in me (only by school kids, never by Mum and Dad) that being gay was bad. But as a teenager, I *was* gay – and overweight – with a face full of acne and a mouth of metal train-track braces. So, things weren't stacked in my favour.

My class, dreaded by every teacher, was full of little shits. By contrast, I was a bit of a goody-two-shoes. My homework was on time. I sat at the front. My uniform was correct: pressed, cleaned and fragranced by fabric softener. Of course, I had school-approved pens and pencils, but a set of glitter gel pens completed my stationery.

My friends were mostly the geeks (all way geekier than me!); we definitely weren't the 'cool' kids smoking around the back of the Music block. Naturally, all this, plus my love for the Spice Girls, Steps, B*Witched, and performing on stage, marked me out to the bullies.

A few years later, it got worse. The school was very big on sports, and for PE lessons, the boys' changing area had three bays with showers, toilets and sinks at the end. The 'cool' kids took the furthest bay. Others, good at sports but not part of the 'cool' crowd, took the next. The third bay was filled with geeks and 'inbetweeners' (the sort who always forgot their sports kit).

No one in any of the bays ever made space for me.

I changed on my own, next to the bin, in a little alcove about one foot wide.

As everyone walked out, they had to pass by the bin, single file. Most boys spat on my clothes or threw my bag into the bin. Other times, they'd kick my bag, trying to smash my pencil case or snap my pencils. More than twenty years later, during COVID, my local gym used these school changing rooms while their own were closed. Reluctantly walking back in, I was transported straight back to this traumatic period.

Before playing rugby, the PE teacher, Mr Hooker, ordered everyone to do a cross-country run. This was often through mist, rain, and freezing conditions, with wet, horrid mud sticking to your boots. Being chubby, I'd either come last or second from last. I hated the entire experience, but although the run exhausted me, I clocked that the longer it took, the less time I'd have to play rugby! That teacher used humiliation as a tactic, presumably to motivate, and he constantly laid into me. It was just awful. He made me feel like I had no place in sports; this feeling sticks with me to this day.

Older bullies took great pleasure in tormenting me. To escape, I'd leave the Dinner Hall as quickly as possible. In the canteen, you could buy hotdog-shaped sugary doughnuts with cream in the middle and strawberry sauce drizzled on top. One day, I was sitting with my performing friends when a bully called Neil came by. He'd spent his entire lunch money on six doughnuts, scooping out the whipped cream and sauce into his hand. As he walked behind me, Neil pretended to slip, smacking all that cream and sauce right in my face.

Yeah. That made me feel pretty shit.

Of course, the entire Dinner Hall roared with laughter, celebrating what Neil had done. My friends completely ignored him, the girls switching into 'mothering' mode, cleaning me up and getting me out. Two days later, Mrs Wyles took me aside and asked why I hadn't reported this incident. To be honest, I reported hardly anything which happened. This infuriated Mrs Wyles as she genuinely wanted to help, but I felt really threatened by Neil, who also bullied my brother Karl a fair bit as well.

Of course, it continued. A banana was thrown down on me from the top of the science block; tea bags were emptied into my hair; I was tripped up by hockey sticks on the pitch. I've blocked out most of the other experiences.

My defence mechanism was comedy. If I could laugh or make a joke, it was a few seconds less they could call me names! And all this just made me more determined to carry on. *Sod, you!* I'd internally yell at the bullies. Never at any point did they make me feel that I shouldn't be a performer or that anything I did wasn't normal. Never! It thrilled me to be in the choir, school productions and operatic society. Here, I was in control of the laughs; people knew it was okay if *I* was making the joke.

And every cloud has a silver lining because it was, in fact, the bullies who brought my best friend into my life.

Emma Donnelly had joined Toot Hill after I arrived. I'd seen her around as we caught the same bus. She lived in her own fun little world, wearing kooky floor-length coats, with funky coloured hair and lots of make-up. Emma was, however, one of the smokers with the 'cool' kids behind the Music block, and she dated a skateboarder.

It was 1997. I was in Year Nine, and the Spice Girls had just released 'Who Do You Think You Are?'. At the end of the summer term, there was a charity day. Everyone paid 50p to wear their own clothes, and pupil-organised talent shows were held in classrooms (known as 'House Rooms'). The setup was basic. No microphones, just a ghetto blaster with a few speakers. My friends encouraged me to do something; as I had the Spice Girls' single cassette with me, I decided to perform their 'Who Do You Think You Are?' dance. With hindsight, this was a very naïve decision: it was the last day of term, and all my bullies would be in the same room.

The kids organising the talent show placed me last, after a girl singer named Tiffany. Being one of the cool kids, everyone arrived to see her. She finished her number – 'Killing Me Softly' – to big cheers.

'We've got one more act now,' someone announced. 'It's Ross, and he's going to dance to the Spice Girls.' That caused a bit of a stir. I stood next to the ghetto blaster. My friends sat down at the front, just to my right. The room was packed, with people standing on tables right at the back...including my bullies.

'Who Do You Think You Are?' blasted out as I danced. Sadly, the fact that I performed the exact routine the right way round (as practised in my mirror) was wasted on this ill-informed crowd. By the middle of the first verse, people were giggling, others outright laughing. Then they started throwing things at me. Screwed up pieces of paper, then pencils and erasers. By the chorus, it was penny-sweets from a tuckshop bag. Some of the sweets hit me, but not in the face. When everything was gone, they chucked the bag. At this point, Emma says she remembers flying sausage rolls. I don't remember that, but Emma swears by it, as her beautiful suede jacket was destroyed by sausage roll juice!

By the middle of the number, somebody had returned from the bathroom with water balloons. They threw a good two or three. Amazingly, none of them hit me. I remained bone dry and was still dancing. At that point, Emma stood up in the middle of the room. She looked gorgeous with her bright red hair, wearing that suede burgundy jacket down to the floor with fur around the collar. Proper retro funk.

'Just leave him alone!' she shouted. 'Let him do what he wants to do!' Well, the bullies still had about three water balloons spare. And who did they throw them at now? Soaked, Emma fled to the bathroom to dry off.

I finished the song with full Girl Power. Immediately after, the school bell rang, and everyone ran out. As I passed by where the cyclists left their bikes, I heard a voice shouting, 'Ross! Ross!'

'Yes?' I asked, turning round.

'I don't know you,' said my new friend. 'But I'm Emma. I think you're really cool, and I'd like to get to know you better.'

A quarter of a century later, our friendship bracelets are engraved with the words 'Who Do You Think You Are?'

King Herod in Jesus Christ Superstar with my dancers, on the far right is Melanie, now I'm Godfather to her son Frankie

Feeling 'Fruity' in the 6th Form Pantomime as 'Ronson'

Far left, as Fredrich in The Sound Of Music, *with Bingham Amateur Dramatics Society*

My brothers 18th Birthday celebration, a rare teen picture of me due to my acne

Center stage at one of the many variety shows at Toot Hill

3. 'AT THE END OF THE TUNNEL, THERE'S A GLIMMER OF LIGHT'

I was 12 when my paternal grandfather died; that's when I first experienced grief. Seeing Grandad cold and lifeless in an open casket, I felt heartbreak. Then, we immediately suffered another loss. Mum left home for a while. Days later, when I got back from Grandad's funeral, the house felt dead and empty. All Mum's things were gone.

The next day was my 13th birthday. Today, people ask, 'Why do you make such a big fuss about your birthday?' Well, it's because I don't want to remember all this *other* stuff which happened. Only years later did I begin to enjoy my birthday.

As we'd never taken foreign holidays with Mum to cheer us up, Dad now went out of his way to give us that experience. My first time abroad was in – wait for it – Benidorm. It was a cheap, no-frills week. Dad kept pulling my leg, saying he'd buy us tickets for an adult performer named Sticky Vicky. Just from the name alone, dear reader, you can imagine the style of act for which she was famed! However, to my horror, Dad really *did* get tickets. I was frogmarched to watch Sticky Vicky, utterly shocked as from her nether regions she produced, Mary Poppins style from a small package, large items culminating in a fully illuminated lightbulb! If I didn't know I was gay before, I certainly did after.

Soon after, Mum returned home. She and Dad were happily reunited, like young lovers all over again. From then on, we took holidays abroad all together, of which I have very fond memories.

In Sixth Form, there's a culture of friends taking foreign holidays. My friend Louise said, 'My cousin lives in San Francisco, near where they filmed *Dawson's Creek*. Do you want to join me to go and visit?' I leapt at the chance, and we both started saving our money.

Then 9/11 happened. Suddenly, airfares and hotels were crazily reduced. Louise's mum handled our advance booking for 2002: three weeks in San Francisco and a week in New York. I arranged with Louise's mum to pay her back in instalments but did everything without telling Mum and Dad. They weren't too happy! My parents paid back Louise's mum, and I had to pay *them* back in instalments. Later, they gave me a New York sightseeing book and $100 spending money. Apart from that, they said this was my trip, and I could sort everything myself.

The holiday was fantastic. It made me realise there was a big world out there, and now that I'd left school, this world was my oyster. We travelled to LA and the Hollywood Hills. In New York, we saw the newly opened *Spiderman* movie (not yet released in the UK) and *Mamma Mia!* on Broadway. That was the hottest ticket in town, but attainable as audiences were down after 9/11. On a city bus tour, we drove past Ground Zero, though it was something neither Louise nor I had wanted to see. I couldn't look. It was still just a hole in the ground. Years later, I revisited to properly pay my respects.

Holidays aside, by now, more than ever, I wanted to be a performer. In my last year of A Levels, I'd attended loads of auditions for TV talent shows – I had decided to become a pop star! Mum and Dad drove me to the nearest audition venues in Birmingham and Manchester, staying overnight in hotels. I always sang 'Love Changes Everything' (one of Mum's favourites) but never got through to see the judges. There were so many rounds, interviews, and workshops beforehand most people got cut and sent home. I quickly realised that this audition process wasn't just about vocal ability. Physical appearance came first. Did you look the part? You can teach someone to sing, but you can't teach a 'look'.

The only non-performing route I ever considered – very briefly – was design for TV. I attended an Open Day for a course at Nottingham Central Studios. They showed a model of a TV set with a little cardboard cutout of a man in front of an audience. But I thought *I don't want to design the sets. I want to be that man, right there, standing on the stage!* My ambition was to be in the spotlight – not behind it.

Then I heard about a job called a Butlin's Redcoat. Loads of mothers from school had encouraged this, saying I'd be perfect. As I didn't do any research, I naively thought that being a Redcoat was the *only* thing I could do and that Butlin's was the *only* place I could work. It became my sole focus. Redcoat auditions, however, weren't until September/October. While I waited, I worked three jobs.

One was for my new godparents. I say new because, at 19, I'd only just been christened (I'd recommend this to anyone – the gifts are amazing). My ceremony took place in Tithby Church on my parents' 25th wedding anniversary, combined with my parents renewing their vows; again, I sang 'Love Changes Everything'.

Being an adult, I'd been able to choose my godparents: our family friends, Karl and Sharon Bartsch. They ran four pubs across Nottinghamshire, and at 16, Sharon had given me my first paid singing gig. I performed at her 40-seat restaurant on Greek-themed Wednesdays. However, I wasn't singing to backing tracks. Oh no. I sang along with actual CDs over someone else's vocals! It was like 'Carpool Karaoke', but worse. Nevertheless, Sharon, bless her, still paid me.

Now age 19, I earned £3.50 an hour as Sharon's waiter. That was a whopping 50p extra than my last job washing dishes at a hotel. It paid for my music purchases and driving lessons (I took 150 before passing; they're called bumpers for a reason, aren't they?!).

In addition, I worked at Asda supermarket. Sometimes, I was on checkout, but in the kiosk, I sold cigarettes and lottery tickets, singing along to hits on our in-house radio station, Asda FM. Sometimes, I was a 'greeter', with a Britney Spears-style headset, microphone, and a massive yellow badge declaring *Happy To Help*. What I loved most was making announcements: 'Here in store, it's Bargains Galore!' But I managed just one shift on the Customer Service Desk. Apparently, I was too generous with refunds and gave away too much money!

Lastly, I worked at a Nottingham nightclub called Jumping Jacks, which had live entertainment from visiting acts. In addition, Jacks Crew (the staff) performed dance routines in costume. We did 'Tragedy' (by Steps) in long white PVC jackets, 'Don't Stop Moving' (by S Club 7) in trendy outfits, and the nights ended with 'Never Forget' (by Take That) wearing silk shirts. I felt invincible, learning to work up a crowd (inebriated on WKD) and letting my pop fantasies run wild!

Finally came my Redcoat audition, for which I had to prepare two songs: an uptempo number and a ballad. Mum and Dad drove me to Skegness with my karaoke CDs as backing tracks. My upbeat song was NSYNC's 'Pop' and my ballad, yet again, 'Love Changes Everything' (the soundtrack of my life at this point).

Our results would arrive by post. I sat by the letterbox for ten days. Then it came. Enclosed was a cardboard oblong with the Butlin's logo and three printed boxes, one of which had a tick, revealing your result. The first box said, 'Congratulations, you've been selected!' The second was, 'We'll keep your information on file.' The third, 'Sorry, you've been unsuccessful.' For me, they'd ticked the second box. I was heartbroken. Really and truly upset. Then, I pulled myself together and kept busy with my jobs.

Soon after, at Jumping Jacks, I worked a night when it was dead as a doornail. However, two ladies came up and asked, 'Have you ever thought about working at Butlin's?'

'Oh yeah,' I replied nonchalantly, 'I've already auditioned. They said they'd keep my stuff on file.'

'Well,' one of the ladies continued, 'We're on a roadshow scouting for Butlin's crew. Now, admittedly, we're looking for all the staff *other* than Redcoats, but tomorrow, one of the Redcoat hires will be at our recruiting event. Why don't you come along and meet him? From what I've seen tonight, I think you'd be great!'

Naturally, I got my hopes up, dressed in my new Topman outfit, and practised my 'welcome' speech. Quelle, Surprise, I didn't get the job.

By now, I had a full-time position at Jumping Jacks, so I'd given up Asda and Sharon's restaurant. As our resident DJ had recently left, replacements arrived every week. For me, this was fantastic; I absorbed everything they did, learning from lots of different people.

When a DJ named Mike arrived, he watched me perform and asked, 'What are you doing here?'. I thought he was being rude, but then he added, 'Why are you doing *this* when you could be doing so much *more?* I've just been working at a Haven holiday camp. You'd be brilliant there!' *What?* I thought to myself. *You mean there's places* other *than Butlin's?!* As I mentioned, this possibility had never crossed my mind. Mike got me signed to an agency called Excellent Entertainment, which promised to let me know if any 'coat' jobs came up.

I loved working at Jumping Jacks, but eventually, due to constant management changes, my job no longer brought me joy, so I handed in my resignation. Asda welcomed me back with open arms in the belief that I'd stay for a lifetime … but all that was about to change.

About two weeks later, I caught the bus home and found Mum waiting at the stop. She was white as a sheet.

'You have to leave your job.'

'Why?!'

'You've had a call from Great British Holiday Parks. They need you down there next week.'

I'd been offered work in Camber on the south coast. It was a six-week trial, and the agency had booked me as an emergency replacement; someone had dropped out (little did I realise then just how often this would happen in my career).

I should have been over the moon, but I wasn't. I felt guilty about Asda, but after a pep talk from Mum, I knew I had to chase my dream. Things moved so fast that I had to send Mum back to Asda with my uniform. I was already packed and off to the Great British Holiday Parks!

I arrived in Camber on a Friday. Just me, my little blue suitcase, and a heartful of dreams. I had no geographical idea where I was and the tiniest amount of money in my pocket. And I loved it. I loved every single second.

My managers, Martin and James, were in charge of schedules. It was all so exciting! I'd jump around celebrating, 'I'm on Late Night Karaoke till three in the morning! Yaaaay!' However, I learned fast that Martin and James gave themselves the best jobs. After nine o'clock at night, no one else had a hope of getting anywhere near that microphone. Still, I relished whatever I was assigned: bouncy castle at 10 a.m. on the dance floor, children's party time at 6 p.m., selling bingo tickets …

Whenever I hosted quizzes, I made sure that everyone knew who I was. I loved trying to make the prizes (leftovers from the arcade grabber machines) sound like the best prizes in the world! And as for playing 'Dillon the Dinosaur' in a life-sized skin costume, well, let's just say I had the time of my life as a very mischievous dinosaur.

My six-week trial whizzed by, but no one hinted whether I'd be staying. During the sixth week, I saw that I was scheduled for the day after my deadline. I didn't get to see Martin until late at night, and I was terrified. Heart pounding, I meekly asked, 'I just wanted to check something. I'm scheduled until the end of the month, but this date is past my six-week trial. Does that mean you would like me to stay?'

'Oh yeah,' Martin said, really blasé. 'Of course, you're staying.'

I was on top of the world!

We performed a show entitled *Legends*. At the time, I thought it was outstanding. With hindsight, my pride was misguided! The show was about deceased music icons: Roy Orbison, Marc Bolan, Karen Carpenter, and Marilyn Monroe. Cast members appeared as each 'legend' singing one of their songs. After each number, the band played Queen's 'Who Wants To Live Forever?' and two Angels (with tinsel halos and white masks) appeared from the wings, walking down caravan steps, escorting each 'legend' back up to Heaven. Those rusty steps were covered with white sheets (old ones no longer used for the guests as they had too many holes).

The finale was me as Elton John singing 'Candle In The Wind', pretending to play a grand piano (which was actually a large circular table with a plank of wood and another set of holey white sheets draped over it). Behind me was a projected slideshow of Princess Diana. Towards the end of the song, I got up and stood centre stage while the 'ghosts' came down from Heaven in white masks, carrying tealights. On the final line of my song, the 'ghosts' lifted their masks and blew out the candles ... and that was the end of the show.

I made great friends with Lisa, the band singer, and on our day off we travelled to London. This was a major deal for me, especially as, with my own earnings, I bought a ticket to see Michael Ball in *Chitty Chitty Bang Bang* at the Palladium. An even bigger deal, however, was that I'd been asked to perform my debut solo show in the holiday park's Stardust Lounge, so in London, Lisa helped me pick my outfit.

My show was billed towards the end of the season when just the chalet and caravan owners were left: a small but mighty crowd! It was the first and only time in my career that I didn't prepare an encore. I learned from this experience; now I've always got one more song in my arsenal. My show was filled with current pop hits – Will Young and Gareth Gates numbers – and I've no doubt it was absolutely terrible. My links between songs were certainly all over the place. But that show was *mine,* and I was very, very proud.

In the meantime, Mum and Dad arrived to help decorate my dated chalet. They gave it an extreme makeover, scrubbing everything out, laying a new carpet, redoing the bathroom, buying new bedding and rugs to throw over the sofa.

Afterwards, they decided to visit as paying guests, booking a holiday around my birthday. As their chalet was very compact, every day, Mum had to position herself in a slightly different way than usual when she was washing under her arms.

That's when she found a lump.

She had it tested.

Mum was told she had breast cancer.

State Side for the first time at 17 years old

Always on the microphone, back in the early 2000's at Jumpin' Jacks

Mum and Dad back together and happier than ever

4. 'THERE'S ONE MORE STAR IN THE SKY'

Holiday park employment was, of course, very seasonal. So, when the Camber contract ended, I went home.

That's when Mum told me. In the kitchen, with Dad there.

In my young, naive brain, I instantly thought, *Oh my God, Mum's gonna die.* I panicked; I was about to lose her immediately. I didn't realise this was just the start of a seven-year journey of different treatments, different drugs and learning to live with cancer.

Mum's lump was the size of a nectarine, so it wasn't an option to simply cut it out or have radiotherapy. She enjoyed a few years of good health and others not so good. But as my career progressed, Mum was there to support me at every level and juncture.

There was one thing which Mum never, ever wanted me to see, and in this, she succeeded: I never saw her in a hospital bed. I think that's partly why I still have so many happy memories; they're not clouded by that image. That's not to say I didn't see her looking poorly at home. As years went by, she had an operation to remove her breast and needed to wear wigs.

Yet, not once did she want our lives to change because of her illness. A few years down the line, I'd been asked to sign up for a second contract working on cruise ships. However, I sat Mum down and said, 'I'm not going back. I'm going to stay on land to be here for you. I want to be your carer.' She was *livid!*

'You are *not* doing that!' she told me. 'You get back on those ships and do what you're meant to be doing! I'll support you, and I'll be there on that ship to cheer you on!' And she was. She came on my ships several times as a guest.

Mum hated being 'Jean the Cancer Victim' and never wanted to look or act like that. In hospital, she made friends with the cleaners who looked after her ward, bonding with one in particular. On the day Mum was discharged, she dressed up very smartly, with perfect make-up and wig. Then she went to find her friend to say goodbye, but the cleaner didn't recognise her. She thought Mum was a visitor. 'You do not look like Mrs Jean!' the cleaner cried, which Mum loved.

In June 2010, my ship was cruising around Italy. I asked my boss for a week's compassionate leave, which was granted. Seven days before I was due home, late during the night of the 24th, I returned to my cabin after hosting a Welcome Party. Literally, as the ship began pulling away, my phone rang. The ringtone was 'Mama' by the Spice Girls, the song I'd allocated Mum. But when I answered, it was Dad's voice.

'She's gone,' he said.

'What?'

'She's gone. Your mum's just gone. She's gone.'

By now, we'd set sail. The ship was barely five metres from the dock, but there was no turning back.

I didn't know how to process Mum's death, but my amazing boss, Mark Dixon, told me that he'd sort everything I needed. My Assistant Cruise Director, Chris, and his girlfriend, Gemma, were equally as supportive. The next day, I stayed in my cabin. Finally, I was able to disembark and fly home from our next port, Palermo in Sicily. To this day, I have no idea how everyone managed to get me back.

Dad and my Uncle Geoff (Mum's brother) picked me up from Heathrow. On the back seat of the car was a Funeral Directors' catalogue.

The drive to Nottingham was three hours, and after seeing my grandparents, Dad had arranged for me to visit other friends and family … but I wanted time for myself.

During her final days, Mum stayed in my room as my bed was slightly higher than hers. Mum's clothes were still hanging over my furniture. As a final Mother's Day present, I'd bought her a silver Tiffany necklace with a heart-shaped padlock.

It was hanging on the top of my dresser.

That's when my heart broke, and I wept.

During the lead-up to the funeral, I was overwrought. I became demanding and difficult, obsessed with planning the day and trying to focus my mind. I felt nothing was good enough for Mum. Everything about the service had to be bright and colourful. We gave her a pink casket. Even the white horses transporting her to the church in a carriage wore pink ribbons.

During the service, I sang 'The Letter' from *Billy Elliot the Musical.* It was a show that Mum and I had seen together in

London … every year while she was ill, Dad had paid for us to have a West End outing. In 'The Letter', Billy reads a message from his late mum. Across the stage, the spirit of Billy's mum sings what she's written. As Mum and I sat there blubbering, she turned to me and said, 'If anything happens to me, *that's* what I'd say to you, your brother and your dad.'

Karl sang Coldplay's 'Fix You', the song he most associated with Mum. Everyone in the church began singing it with him, even older relatives I thought would never have even heard of Coldplay.

Mum is buried under a tree close to her childhood family home. Funnily enough, she's next to the vicar who married her and my dad. Her plot had to be paid for in cash. The moment we handed it over, Grandad put his hand in his pocket and pulled out more money.

'And I,' he announced, 'Want the spot next to her.'

That broke my heart even more. At that precise moment, I couldn't even contemplate further loss.

Mum's headstone was specially designed. It has a hand-carved mini sculpture of a ladybird crawling over the top, as that was her nickname. All along the sides are words describing Mum. We each chose something to express what she meant to us. My word didn't fit, so we placed it on the footing of the stone: 'Inspirational'.

I was 26 when we lost Mum, and it really cemented my belief in making memories. I truly feel that making memories is something I must do because that's what Mum did for us. The reason I'm obsessed with Christmas and Easter is because she made them special. If I don't keep that love and energy alive, what was the point of Mum going to all that effort?

I still don't know if I've ever properly processed Mum's death. My grief has been very private. I won't discuss it, mention it in my shows, or post about it on social media. I respect that, for other people, public expressions can help, but it's not for me.

Today, on ships, sometimes guests assume I still have both parents: 'Your mum must be so proud'. And I've no doubt she was ... and is. I feel very fortunate that I don't ever question that. One of Mum's favourite things was to be recognised as 'Ross' Mum'. If anyone stopped her and asked, 'Are you Ross' Mum?', her chest swelled with pride. 'Yes, I *am!* she smiled. 'I *am* Ross' Mum!' So, nor do I question how much Mum loved me or whether she knew how much I loved her.

As we shall see, several years after she passed, I had to move on from my first cruise company. Sometimes, I still wonder if I stayed there too long. But at the time, I genuinely worried that if I left, Mum wouldn't know where I'd gone. Eventually, I realised this was silly ... because, of course, she's around me all the time.

Everyone's going to say their mum was amazing. But mine really was.

One of my favourite photographs of mum and me, off to London to see a west end show, given as a gift from Dad.

5. 'COULD BE A BIG SUCCESS'

But now, back to 2003...

Having realised that different holiday parks existed, I wanted to crack the audition circuit. I attended an open call in Stratford-Upon-Avon for Haven Holidays, a non-stop day of one-on-one meetings and workshops.

In a group dance call, we learned a routine to 'Gold' by Spandau Ballet; on the final beat of the music, everyone dropped to one knee. We danced for the panel in groups of four, and as my group dropped to our knees, I heard the mightiest sound of ripped material. *Oh gosh,* I thought, *Somebody's had an accident!* As I stood up, I felt material rubbing my leg. Then I clocked that my denim jeans felt rather loose in between my legs. Finally, my hand reached down and felt bare thigh. *Ohhhh no! It's me!* From underneath the fly, all the way up to the belt loops at the back, the entire seam had gone.

Afterwards, sitting in a circle, everyone had to share 'one interesting fact about yourself which nobody else knows.'

'Hi everybody,' I began, 'My name is Ross. I travelled down from Nottingham today, and I'm going to share something with you that's just happened, actually. I've split my trousers open.' I stood up and turned around. 'Is it bad?' I asked coquettishly, wiggling my bum. The entire room rolled on the floor, laughing. It became a running joke, and during a 'hosting' audition, I tied my hoody around my front, the best position for fuller coverage. Haven Holidays offered me a job in Blackpool but as something called a 'Fun Star'. This meant no singing was involved. That wasn't ideal, but I accepted the job.

The very next day, I received a phone call from my Camber friend Sally. She was rehearsing at Pontins Pakefield in Lowestoft, and one of their boys had just dropped out. 'Can you come here tomorrow and audition?' she asked. 'I've told them about you, and they're excited to see you!'

At a private audition, for the first time ever, the panel let me sing both my numbers all the way through: 'Love Changes Everything' and, would you believe it, 'Gold'! They rang and asked me to start immediately, a job with singing included. Once again, I'd been offered work because someone had dropped out.

Of course, I wanted to say yes, but then I remembered Mum's long-standing advice. Years before, when I'd been offered 'Friedrich' in *The Sound of Music,* I'd accepted the part then and there. But Mum said, 'Don't always accept things straight away. Always make them wait and say, "Can I get back to you?"' So, I did make Pontins wait a short time, which allowed me to sort things with Haven.

Pontins was a step up from Camber – they fully rehearsed their shows! They also had proper branding, and in my beautiful blue coat, I felt totally professional. The downside was a minimal salary, out of which I paid chalet rent and covered food costs. Mum, unimpressed, called it 'survival money'. Once again, Mum and Dad arrived to perform a 'Laurence Llewellyn-Bowen' transformation on my meagre new home.

What I learned at Pontins was priceless. I absorbed the art of hosting, leading quizzes and bingo in the main ballroom and Princess Bar. As a late-night host, I got away with all sorts, including risqué jokes!

I learned a great deal from an Entertainment Manager named Graham Henry, a legend of Pontins Pakefield. A constant smoker, he'd run 'Cigarette Raffles'. Every chalet wrote their number on a cigarette, handed over to Graham. He'd make the draw and give away a prize, but then he kept and smoked all the cigarettes, about 500 of them!

Graham made everything entertaining. Bingo wasn't just a game; it was his own stand-up comedy show. He cracked brilliant jokes, properly constructed with a beginning, middle and end. Granted, they were all stolen from Guest Entertainers, but everyone, me included, ate it up. Graham Henry was a huge influence, and I have nothing but love and respect for the man and his career.

Pakefield really invested in entertainment and occasionally brought in two veteran celebrity comedians, Mick Miller and Bernie Clifton. They'd both enjoyed illustrious careers, so I volunteered to work their spotlight; it shook me because I laughed so much! I also watched other Guest Entertainers. Many used the same material, so I'd analyse what made one performer get a bigger laugh than the other.

I learned about stage presence and technique. I was never a huge fan of singers who clasped their microphone stands like a crutch throughout their numbers. Nor did I like awkward silence while they drank a glass of water. Others handled technical mishaps better than others. I applied everything I learned to my revised solo show, and, of course, I'm *still* learning to this day.

After promotion to Chief Host, I received a call from my Jumping Jacks friend Donna: 'I'm currently working on a cruise ferry, and one of the boy singers has dropped out. Are you available to come to London this weekend and audition?'

By coincidence, I was already heading to London that weekend. We'd been given time off, so my bluecoat friend Lindsay and I were headed to my first London gay bar. When I told her about the audition, though, she insisted, 'You've got to go!'

The company was called Live Business, and my audition was at a church hall in East Putney. I sang 'Empty Chairs At Empty Tables' all the way through, which I took as a good sign. But the moment I finished, a lady on the panel, Debbie Blackett, opened her flip phone and made a call. I was just standing there while she spoke to someone, all the while looking at my CV (or resumé, for American readers). That, I assumed, was a bad sign. I waited for her to finish and then went to leave.

'Thank you so much for seeing me.'

'Where do you think you're going?' Debbie suddenly asked.

'Oh,' I cried, startled. 'I just assumed it hadn't gone very well.'

'You're not what *I'm* looking for,' she replied, 'But I like the look of your CV. I've just spoken to a gentleman named Dave

Taylor, and I'd like you to go to our Head Office and talk to him.'

Head Office was around the corner on Calico Row, for which they gave verbal directions. Well, could I find it? It took 45 minutes! Eventually, when I got there, Dave Taylor kept me talking for an hour. I was flabbergasted. He offered me the job of Entertainment Manager on board a ferry! I'd be in charge of the very team of ten performers for which I'd just auditioned. Then I remembered Mum's advice to wait before accepting a job. Dave told me, 'You've got until lunchtime tomorrow.'

I said yes.

My six-month trial with Live Business aboard The Pride of York went very well. We sailed between Hull and Zeebrugge. The stability of this repeated schedule, including days off in Hull, was comforting. If there was an emergency with Mum, I could always get back home.

The salary, in comparison to Pontins, was incredible, and Hull, in comparison to Lowestoft, was a metropolis! I joined my first-ever gym. At this point, I was big ... about a 48-inch waist. I did my best to lose weight, but that didn't work; after every trip to the gym, I rewarded myself with a visit to the bakery!

On the ferry, many guests made illegal tobacco runs. Every Thursday and Friday, a family crossed with a minibus. Eventually, they were caught smuggling a tonne of tobacco hidden inside. In Hull, I saw a trendy couple, with whom I'd bantered during a quiz, caught red-handed with several huge duffel bags of tobacco – Hull's answer to Pablo Escobar!

As for my job, though, I was in charge. I could make all my own decisions about the entertainment. One time, Mum and Dad came aboard (how Mum managed this, I'll never know; she had terrible seasickness and motion sickness). That day, in my 'Name That Tune' quiz, I changed three songs to numbers, which they'd heard me perform countless times. And how many points do you think my parents scored, dear reader? Big fat zero!

After three months on *The Pride of York*, Dave Taylor announced I was earmarked to work on a new cruise ship – not a ferry – a proper cruise ship – called *Island Star*. This ship was owned by Royal Caribbean and First Choice (later sold to Thomson Travel Group), but Live Business handled all their entertainment. As Chief Host, I'd lead a team of five. Before we launched *Island Star*, however, my team was offered a transatlantic crossing on her sister ship, *Island Escape*. This allowed us to run all our material, including the gameshows.

Afterwards, we began our nine-month contract aboard *Island Star*. During this time, my job title changed from Chief Host to Venue Manager. I was thrilled about that; I felt elevated and that I had a venue of which to be in charge!

Working on ships was far more regimented than working on land. In holiday camps, I'd done anything and everything asked of me. At sea, we *had* to stick purely to performing. I especially focused on developing my own show. On cruise ships, I found it wasn't unusual for guests to walk out during a performance, and I noticed they decided either to stay or leave during the second song. So, I *had* to win them over by the start of my second number. I began constantly experimenting with the material – putting songs in, taking songs out – and crafting the right balance.

I also discovered that working at sea was not just a job. It was a lifestyle. And it was a lifestyle I absolutely loved. On *Island Star*, I watched and learned what the role of the Cruise Director entailed. I very quickly decided that, ultimately, *this* was the job for me. Now, my greatest ambition was to become a Cruise Director. So, you can imagine my excitement at what happened next.

During *Island Star*'s final fortnight, in addition to being Venue Manager, I had to step in as Assistant Cruise Director. He'd been offered panto with one of the Nolan Sisters and was being released early. But then, sadly, his father passed away unexpectedly, so I became ACD for six weeks rather than two.

I loved the challenge of having two jobs, being constantly busy, and giving my all. This led to my promotion as a full-time ACD aboard *Island Escape*. For this opportunity, I must thank two of the stalwarts of Live Business, Mark Dixon and Dave Taylor. Looking ahead, I would never have become a Cruise Director for Seabourn at the age that I did without such great early boosts from Mark and Dave.

Throughout those two years as ACD, Mum booked several cruises as a guest. During my show, when the audience sang along with 'Sweet Caroline', she was the only person in the room clapping out of time. When I mentioned this, Mum explained, 'Oh, I'm so focused on what *you're* doing, I can't work out what my *hands* are doing at the same time!' It was one of the cutest things she ever said.

My Cruise Director was Gary Rawlings. He and his partner Stuart are still my great friends to this day. Knowing that I wanted to become a Cruise Director myself, Gary was kind and secure enough to nurture this passion. During my two years as Gary's ACD, I sensed him subconsciously preparing me for that eventual call offering promotion if it ever came.

And it *did*. In 2008, at the age of 25.

There had been an emergency over on *Island Star*. Live Business needed a replacement Cruise Director immediately and sent Gary. That, in turn, meant that *Island Escape* now required a new Cruise Director.

We were in Palma de Mallorca when Mark Dixon rang and offered me a promotion. I'll tell you this, dear reader ... I definitely did *not* ask him, 'Can I get back to you?'. I let Mark know immediately that I was accepting the job. I wanted this! I *wanted* this!

I was a Cruise Director!

I wanted to run up to the funnel and scream at the top of my lungs!

I was so proud and overwhelmed.

It was the start of everything to come...

Pontins Bluecoat, so proud to have mum and dad there with me

Entertainment Manager on the Pride of York...yes i know - the shirt was a not my best fashion choice!

Later years and mum and me in the markets of France during an Island Escape cruise

6. 'SHA LA LA ... YOU'RE DOING FINE!'

Everything happened instantly. I didn't even have anything to wear as Cruise Director! It was embarkation day – our busiest day of the week – so my friend Sarah Jane and I had to run – actually run – all through Palma de Mallorca to buy me a suit from Zara. This first gorgeous grey outfit made me feel totally professional and inspired my affinity with jackets and blazers. Having struggled with weight my entire life, I loved their flattering fits.

Then I had to move cabins. To this day, my *Island Escape* cabin was the biggest I've ever had. Once I'd done it up, it was like a mini apartment, but I was so busy I spent hardly any time there. That first evening, introduced over the microphone as 'Your Cruise Director', I had goose pimples. The tech team asked if I wanted to change my regular entrance music, but I kept what I'd had as ACD, the most dramatic instrumental moment from 'Dreamgirls'.

On my first day, there was great energy about the ship, with colleagues offering lots of support. But very quickly, the dynamic of certain relationships shifted. As my promotion to Cruise Director happened mid-season, several people had trouble adjusting to me being in charge. Individuals I'd considered friends now backed off quite considerably. That was a hard lesson to learn, and I felt very lonely. On the flip side, it became difficult when I met amazing new people

79

whom I wanted to befriend but couldn't. If I got too close, I might have been accused of favouritism.

However, I'm very glad that on *Island Escape,* I was able to help many people working at sea for the first time. Some eventually became Cruise Directors themselves. If I have helped, supported, or inspired them during their journeys, I feel very proud.

Thomson offered *Island Escape* cruises for nine months of the year, starting and ending with transatlantic voyages. Otherwise, the rest of the time, we sailed around the Mediterranean. Then, during winter, the ship was chartered around Brazil. At that point, *Island Escape* became a proper Party Ship. Although I wasn't Cruise Director for these charters (they took place during my months off), I was always on board for their last few weeks. This was because I had to rehearse with my team, setting everything up for the British season. It was a pure hedonistic festival atmosphere. The things I saw!

One of the Brazilian cruises was Ministry of Sound themed. I left the party at two in the morning, at which point there were, I believe, several wandering hands in the hot tub (that's all I'll say … not to mention certain escapades in the pool). When I got up for breakfast at half past eight, everyone I'd left on deck six hours earlier was still there, dancing away.

Of course, I watched the Brazilian shows in the theatre. If a favourite song was performed, everyone got up and danced. They weren't drunk; this was just the general energy of the cruise. In fact, on these charters, we had no alcohol-related issues. Brazilians can make a whole bottle of vodka last an entire evening; they don't need a drink to have a good time.

The atmosphere at deck parties was infectious, so our officers got involved. Everyone, from the captain down, began performing Crew Dances for the guests. They'd come out doing sexy Latino party moves, and everyone had the best time. From then on, Crew Dances continued throughout the nine-month British season.

Otherwise, the contrast between Brazilian and British cruises was astounding. Literally overnight, everything changed. Instead of piped Brazilian dance music, Petula Clark was on a loop. Bronzed Brazilian bodies vanished. Now, staid older Brits emerged at 6.30 a.m., staking claims with towels on sun loungers.

On that note, in nearly 20 years at sea, I don't think I've ever known a ship to have enough sun loungers. Never. Not once. The number of jokes inspired by sun loungers is just ridiculous. One time on *Island Escape*, I was performing a solo show in front of the pool. The deck was pretty crowded, but just off to my side were two empty sun loungers. Out of my peripheral, I saw two ladies approaching. Instead of walking round the pool to the sun loungers, they decided to walk across my stage while I was singing. But then, they didn't even *sit* on the sun loungers. They just put down their towels and books and walked off back across my stage, in front of me, still singing. I was furious, so I ripped their towels off the sun loungers and chucked them in the pool. It got the biggest cheer of my entire show. People and sun loungers are weirdly territorial; normal rules don't apply!

Naturally, I loved *Island Escape*, but she was an old ship and didn't come without problems. Years later, working for Seabourn, we stopped in *Island Escape*'s old turnaround port, Palma de Mallorca. My Seabourn friend asked whether, back in the day, I'd ever spent an overnight here, to which I replied, 'Only when we had engine failure.'

The state of the ship led to my favourite ever 'overheard' quote. One night, I walked along Deck Five past a cabin with an open door. A mother had asked her teenage son to go to reception and put down a deposit for a hairdryer.

'Ugh,' the teenager sulked. 'Where's reception?'

'It's down that corridor,' she replied. 'Turn right after the second big stain on the carpet.'

Of course, being Cruise Director wasn't all fun and games. On *Island Escape*, I learned to cope with extraordinary circumstances. Throughout my career, when the phone's gone, I've dealt with every scenario you can think of.

'Ross, one of your Kids Club workers has just been washed down by the morning deck-wash crew. She'd passed out on deck last night.'

'Somebody's failed the alcohol test.'

'Somebody's failed the drugs test.'

'Your drummer's been dismissed. He's been disrespectful to the captain.'

'This guy pulled a moony at a guest.'

'This guest has complained; the DJ called her fat and ugly over the microphone.'

'There's raw sewage leaking down the walls backstage, and it's destroyed the feather plumes in the dancers' headdresses!'

'You need to come downstairs. Jason has harmed himself.'

I've dealt with miscarriages, sexual harassment, abortions, bedbugs, people chopping their fingers off, people losing an ear, Guest Entertainers arrested shoreside and locked up as the ship pulls away.

There is never a dull day as a Cruise Director. But nothing could compare to 'The Cruise From Hell'. It was Christmas 2009, sailing round the Canary Islands.

It was awful.

Just Awful.

I will never forget that cruise.

Never ever, ever, ever until the day I die.

One of the guests even registered an official website for it: cruisefromhell.com.

All the mechanics went wrong, and we had engine failure. Then, the plumbing broke, and the toilets burst. In the gents' loos outside the theatre, urinals overflowed. Housekeeping placed towels beneath the urinals to soak it all up (as best they could). Then, we had a massive outbreak of D&V and gastroenteritis. Most of the guests were quarantined, confined to their cabins.

Eventually, a meeting was called in the theatre; the captain addressed the guests, and then the guests aired their views. Can you imagine the atmosphere? And who had to walk around with a microphone for guests to speak their piece? I was a lamb to the slaughter. Not only that, as Cruise Director, it was my responsibility to keep the guests happy throughout this ordeal, which was very tough and challenging. But I shall never forget the utter professionalism of our captain; to this day, we still talk of our ordeal!

Unfortunately, Mum and Dad were on this cruise. Thank God, neither went down with D&V, but of course, this turned out to be Mum's last Christmas. Twelve months later, Dad came on board for Christmas once again. My grandma makes the best mince pies in the world (seriously), so Dad smuggled twelve in his hand luggage for us to enjoy on Christmas morning in my cabin.

As we've seen, Christmas is hugely important to me because of the traditions and memories Mum made for our family. Adjusting to Christmas never being the same took a long time to process. However, in life, you must always move forward. I decided to make new traditions while still acknowledging the old.

One of my new traditions is 'Fake Christmas'. At the time of writing, out of the twelve Christmases since Mum died, I've spent all but two at sea. So, whenever I'm back home, 'Fake Christmas' happens when family comes round for a traditional Christmas Day, but on completely the wrong date. Emotionally, I get my proper Christmas, giving and receiving presents. Then, on the ship, I spend Christmas Day focused entirely on the guests, making their experience perfect. My nephews have told me they actually *prefer* 'Fake Christmas'. Those two seasons I was home for Christmas Day, they were quite disappointed!!

The hosting skills I'd learned at holiday camps now came into their own. As Cruise Director, I hosted loads of gameshows. One of our most popular was 'Mr & Mrs'. One spouse stayed backstage while the other was quizzed about their relationship. Then, their partner came out for the audience to see if their answers matched.

'Where,' this husband was asked, 'Is the most unusual place you've ever got keen and amorous?' He replied that they'd once had fun in a hayfield. Then we brought out his wife and asked her the same question.

'Ohhh,' she pondered. 'I don't know. I can't think of anywhere, really.'

'Nowhere in the countryside, maybe?' At this point, the audience was in stitches. 'Walking back to the car after a picnic? In a hayfield?'

The penny suddenly dropped. The wife exploded, 'That *wasn't with me!!*'

I became well known for my sail-away Welcome Parties on the first night of each cruise. We had gameshows, live music, and sing-alongs for the holiday spirit. *Island Escape* might have been an old ship, but these parties made the guests realise they could still have a great time. This led, however, to perhaps the most surreal moment of my entire career.

In Italy, we held an 'Imaginary New Year Party'. Before midnight, we pretended to be in the 1960s, and after counting down to midnight, we were in the 1970s. I wore an awful vivid '70s top, flared denim jeans and a massive pink frizzy Afro.

As we had a late sail away, the party began while docked at the quayside. Meanwhile, unbeknownst to me, giving my best John Travolta on the dance floor, *Island Escape* had been accused by Italian locals of discharging too much black smoke from our funnel, so now the police came on board. All of a sudden, a Bridge Officer ran across the deck, screaming at me, 'You're needed on the bridge! Urgently! Urgently!'

The captain was there with about fourteen Italian policemen. They had guns in leather thigh straps, and all wore hats. When foreign police wear hats indoors, you know you're in trouble. For some reason, they'd summoned every head of department, all now standing in a line. I was the last to arrive. Each person was quizzed, the police making their way down the line of fully striped, white-uniformed senior officers. Then the SWAT Team got to me: in my flared denim jeans and massive pink frizzy Afro. I answered every question with an entirely straight face, pulling in my cheeks, trying not to smile or roar with laughter!

I loved dressing up. I was a comedy Irish dancer, a ridiculous Greek Olympian, and a dancing Russian bear, with seasonal dress-up for Valentine's, St Patrick's, Easter and more. There was nothing like hearing the deck erupt with laughter. Such a lift in the atmosphere was a huge reward, and I still learned from those around me. *Island Escape* provided first jobs for many of our production singers and dancers straight out of top London drama schools. From them, I absorbed techniques to which I hadn't been exposed, having never officially trained.

Equally, I continued to improve my solo show by watching Guest Entertainers, just as I'd done at holiday parks. Sometimes, we had phenomenally talented singers, dancers, musicians, and magicians, but if their dialogue links between numbers were poor, it killed their entire act. I despaired when people kept saying 'Errrrm…' every few seconds. The links are *just* as important as the main parts of the show, if not more so.

When appropriate, I was happy to pass on this knowledge. A wonderfully talented West End singer came on board whose songs were excellent. But his links – that glue holding the show together – were not as strong. Afterwards, he was good enough to listen to some pointers I offered. When he came back six months later, it was like a completely different show. His songs were the same, but the overall effect and flow, by his own admission, was so much better.

I've genuinely loved giving up-and-coming young talent a chance to shine. It's brought me such great joy. This is something I did from day one because I remembered how much I appreciated my first chances at holiday parks. In later years, I was able to offer a wonderful band musician, Jim Hodgson, the chance to perform his debut solo show. Today, he's taken his production on countless ships, and I'm very proud to have helped open that first door.

However, a very frustrating part of my job was dealing with shipboard management (which I stress was separate from the wonderful Live Business). It was very much revenue-driven over guest experience. I'll never forget a meeting called by the Hotel Director: 'If you didn't wake up this morning and think, *How can I make more revenue than I did yesterday?* This isn't the job for you.' Well, I certainly had not woken up thinking that. I woke up thinking, *How are we going to give the guests a great day and provide good entertainment?*

I gave a lot to my job on *Island Escape*, but internal politics were frustrating. Overall, though, I have hugely fond memories, especially of some amazing guests. In addition, *Island Escape* offered my first proper taste of travel and working with multinational crews. I don't know if I'd have fallen in love with this lifestyle in the way that I did had it not been for *Island Escape*.

2016 marked my eighth year as Cruise Director. At this point, it had been announced that Thomson was selling *Island Escape*. I was informed that if I wished to be considered for other Thomson ships – the entertainment for which, sadly, Live Business did not handle – then I'd have to reapply.

At this time, Live Business had no ships needing Cruise Directors, so I messaged colleagues on other lines, asking if they knew of opportunities. A friend recommended me to a company offering a three-month contract. Sadly, this job was not the right fit for me. I became very disenchanted with the product, but help was at hand …

Live Business gave me a job in Majorca, training young reps for family hotels. I taught everything from kids' party dances to microphone techniques and game shows. One day, Mark Dixon found me dancing behind a screen, purely for my own amusement, improvising moves to the Little Mix song 'Black Magic'.

'Do you think we should make that song one of the party dances this year?' he asked.

'Yes!' I cried.

'Okay,' he replied. 'Put a dance together and perform it tonight.'

It was a race against time, but I choreographed a routine, taught it to the reps, and somehow, magic happened. When we performed, the room erupted. It might have just been a silly little party dance, but in comparison to the all-time low I'd just experienced at my last job, that moment changed everything. I was energised rejuvenated, and knew that I *was* still doing the right thing. Yet again, Live Business had offered a life-affirming opportunity.

This hotel job kept me busy for a while, flying between various locations. Then, in Greece, I received a call from Mark offering a temporary Cruise Director job aboard Saga. I'd met the head of Saga when he'd visited *Island Escape,* and he wanted me to start immediately; their CD had been taken ill. I accepted the job, but then, just hours later, I received an email from a contact named Paul McAvoy. He'd kept my CV on file since I'd left *Island Escape,* and his message said, 'I'll call you in five minutes'.

'I've got you an interview with Seabourn.'

'Sorry, I beg your pardon?'

'I've got you an interview with Seabourn.'

'Okay. When is it?'

'It's a phone interview next week.'

Next week – fine. Enough time to fly out and get settled with Saga.

I enjoyed my time on Saga, although every officer kept reminding me, 'You're only here temporarily, aren't you?' I was quite aware that I'd just been hired as cover, but it became a running joke.

My Seabourn interview with a Senior Manager named Chris Jurasas coincided with the Saga ship leaving Hamburg.

At the precise moment of my transatlantic call, someone on land decided to fire a twelve-cannon salute.

'Hello!' I yelled down the phone, 'Can you hear me?'

'Yes, I can hear you,' Chris replied.

'I just have to tell you before we start,' I bellowed, 'If you hear any gunshots going off, don't worry. I'm not in a war zone. It's just a twelve-cannon salute!' That made Chris howl.

To my amazement, several calls and emails later, I'd been offered a Cruise Director job with Seabourn! It became official on my last night with Saga. But Chris informed me that as I needed extra paperwork to join Seabourn's roster of Cruise Directors, I could spend two weeks in the meantime as one of their ACDs. I was to start just three days later.

The next morning, the Saga cruise was completed. I was at the gangway with my bags when the head of the company dashed up.

'Oh, Ross! I'm so glad I caught you. Do you have a minute for me in the Hotel Director's office?' At that point, after being constantly reminded by every Saga officer that I was there 'temporarily', now I was informed, 'We'd like to make you a permanent member of the Saga family.' I thanked them, albeit hastily adding, 'But I've literally just accepted a job with Seabourn. It was all agreed last night.' Saga was very generous and told me they were delighted for my success.

The entire journey home to Nottingham, I screamed down the phone to my loved ones that I was now a Cruise Director with Seabourn. I could not have been happier!

Aboard my first Seabourn ship – *Odyssey* – something happened, which I took as a sign that I was *meant* to be there.

Several years earlier, my dear friend Jayne Curry had appeared as a Guest Entertainer on a Seabourn charter. She told me, 'The room service is amazing. It even comes with mini tomato ketchup and mini mayonnaise.'

Sometime after, I was out shopping with Jayne. In Selfridges, we saw similar bottles of mini tomato ketchup and mini mayonnaise.

'Ooo,' I said, picking one up. 'Here's your room service!'

'You'll be ordering room service with mini ketchup one day, Ross,' Jayne replied, smiling.

Now, maddeningly, during my first few days aboard *Odyssey*, I came down with D&V. Quarantined in my suite, I ordered room service. And what appeared on my tray? Mini tomato ketchup and mini mayonnaise. I took a picture and texted Jayne, 'My room service has arrived!'

It was one of those wonderful moments where I felt that life had come full circle.

The pink wig, only suitable for Italian Police, with my friend Hayley Jane

*In rehearsals in London for our Hairspray section of the show...obviously I HAD
to try the heels on*

Poolside fun with Yeurgos the Greek Olympian

The final Season of Island Escape, and whole lot of memories

Being Uncle Ross is my favorite job...this was my goodbye hug before I flew to my first Seabourn adventure

We did it Jayne, mini Ketchup bottles!

7. 'CONSEQUENTLY WORKED MUCH HARDER, EVEN WITH DEVOTION'

At my first Seabourn meeting, the Hotel Director asked, 'How are the guests today? What's the atmosphere like on the ship? What can we do to make the guests feel special?'

I knew I'd found my home.

My short stint as ACD was invaluable. Conscious that Seabourn's brand was unique, I wanted to learn. I was in safe hands with Cruise Director David E. Green, who'd been with Seabourn since Day One. I was obsessed with Seabourn pin badges and adored David's. It sparkled, so I assumed it had Swarovski crystals.

'David,' I gushed, 'That is so beautiful. Where can I get one? Do they sell them in the shops?'

'Oh no,' he replied. 'It's got diamonds. This was awarded to me as Employee of the Year after 30 years of service.'

'I'm just hoping to get through *three days* of service!' I howled.

Finally, my paperwork was sorted, and I arrived in Athens as Cruise Director of Seabourn *Sojourn*. But my bags had been lost. I was mortified. How could I present myself with pride for my first Seabourn cruise? I was rescued by a saint named Mary Vargas. She was Port Agent for all the Greek

Islands; in fact, she's the best Port Agent in the world. I don't know how she managed it, but somehow, two days later, in some tiny, weeny, obscure Greek port, Mary awaited with my bags at the quayside. Today, I am proud to call her my dear friend.

I learned on the job what worked and what didn't. For instance, teaching guests the *Zorba* dance in the middle of a toga party killed the atmosphere completely! Yet, while conscious of the Seabourn brand, I still wanted to be me: the 'Ross Cupcake' but with Seabourn icing and sprinkles.

Late one night, up by the Sky Bar, I had a wonderful chat with a guest (whose pastel yellow Chanel handbag I remember to this day). I confided everything I hoped to bring to Seabourn but wondered if the clientele would accept my brand of fun. Or perhaps they'd only want, for instance, a classical string quartet. This wonderful lady dispelled my preconceptions.

'Just because I've got a few extra pounds in my purse,' she told me, 'Doesn't mean that I don't want to have a good time. I still enjoy The Rolling Stones. I still enjoy AC/DC. Yes, I like classical stuff, too. But I still like to have a good time.'

My first contract went well, but I didn't yet feel I was fully 'me'. I continued learning, thrust into covering a two-week filler. Then, Chris asked me to join a holiday cruise over Christmas and New Year. Initially, as a favour, I'd be emergency Cover ACD to David E. Green before taking over as Cruise Director four weeks later (afterwards, my greater understanding of Seabourn ACDs' workload helped future relations with my own ACDs). In addition, I watched how David, a true master, ran a holiday cruise.

Sometime later, David took over from me as Cruise Director in Athens. I met him at the terminal, and as I hugged him, gushed, 'David, you've lost weight!' He made no comment. I had no idea he was ill nor that this would be his last contract. When David passed away, I was devastated but found peace in how fortunate I'd been to know and work with him.

Even now, I still didn't feel entirely 'me', but this changed when Chris Jurasas came on board.

'Do you always introduce the shows off stage?' he asked.

'Well,' I offered, 'I have been on the Seabourn ships, yes.'

'What did you do on your other ships?'

'Oh, I went up and introduced them *on* stage.'

'Well,' he cried, 'Get up there and go on stage!'

That was all I needed.

Gradually, I became known and trusted by Seabourn's valued guests. Totally understandably, guests formed bonds with their Cruise Directors. Therefore, a new face could, sometimes, be a surprise. When I met guests on embarkation day, some looked startled and cried, 'Oh! You're not Handré!'

'No,' I confirmed. 'I'm not Handré.'

'Do you know Handré?' others asked. 'We know Handré very well. We love Handré.'

Of course, they were referring to Seabourn's beloved Cruise Director (and now, at the time of writing, Director of Entertainment & Enrichment), Handré Potgieter.

I love and deeply respect Handré. He is a phenomenal human being, a renowned entertainer, and an incredible Cruise Director. I could not be more honoured to have Handré as my friend. But it was terribly frustrating being constantly told, however well-intentioned, 'Ohhh, you've got big shoes to fill!'

I couldn't be Handré. There is only one Handré. And he already exists. All that I could be was the best Ross that I could be. All that I could do was fill my *own* shoes. So, I was deeply touched when a guest told me, 'When I first met you, I said "Oh! You're not Handré!" And now, I realise that was wrong. Because you're Ross. And I love what you do!'

As time went by, I was thrilled to develop wonderful relationships with our guests, visit parts of the world I'd never seen, and meet incredible VIPs with whom Seabourn had formed official partnerships. I'll never forget when I was told, 'Oh, by the way, you're on with Sir Tim Rice.'

'Sorry,' I said, taking a moment to process this. 'What?!'

I could not believe that I'd be working with Sir Tim Rice, lyricist of my favourite musical, *Joseph And The Amazing Technicolor Dreamcoat*. He'd be on board for sixteen days.

I'm not at all good around famous people, especially my idols. I waffle. Or say the wrong thing. Or act like an idiot *after* I've said the wrong thing. It's like my brain disconnects from my mouth in sheer excitement! However, Sir Tim could not have been more generous. In his Seabourn show, he told wonderful stories about his musicals, songs, and contributions to Oscar-winning films. In private conversation afterwards, I was lucky enough to hear about the new song he'd just written for the upcoming live-action remake of *The Lion King*. I was overwhelmed that this man, whose work had shaped my childhood, was sharing his time with me. But the best was yet to come.

Towards the end of that cruise, I performed my solo show, and back in those days, it took place in the Club rather than the Grand Salon. I was stunned the room was so full; in fact, the show went up late as our Safety Officer had to check whether the Club could hold that many people. The audience's reaction was hugely gratifying. Somehow, that night, everything just clicked, and the stars aligned. Every joke landed. Every song went as well as it could.

Afterwards, I was at the door thanking guests when Sir Tim's PA appeared.

'Tim wants a word with you!'

'I beg your pardon?'

I had no idea that Sir Tim's PA had been in the audience, let alone Sir Tim himself. He was still sitting right at the back of the Club in a corner. As I approached, he stood up, hugged me, and held me by the shoulders in a solid, affirming way.

'Ross,' he told me, 'That was sensational!'

As long as I live, I will never forget that moment. I could have died happy that instant. It still gives me goosebumps.

I wondered if there might be an appropriate time to tell Sir Tim just how much *Joseph* had shaped my life, but I needed to make sure it wouldn't be another brain-disconnecting moment. After his final talk, I joined him on stage to say all the necessary thankyous. That's when I thought *If I don't say it now, I'll never get this chance again, and I'll regret that.*

'When I was a seven-year-old boy,' I announced, 'I went to London to see *Joseph and the Amazing Technicolour Dreamcoat*. It set me off on the path that's led to this day today. In the opening song of that musical, there's a line you wrote which says it's *"the story of a boy whose dreams came true."* And my dream's come true.'

The audience reaction was overwhelming, and I understand that Sir Tim was quite touched, as well. It remains one of the greatest moments of my life. Again, here was another 'full circle' moment offered to me by Seabourn. Only this time, it came with fireworks!

Jazz hands with Sir Tim Rice

Sarah Brightman moments before she sang Happy Birthday

8. 'HIDE ALL THE WORLD FROM ME'

fter three years with Seabourn, I felt like incredible days stretched endlessly ahead.

Until 2020.

On 13th February, I flew to Singapore to join *Ovation*. Touching down on the 15th, my phone lit up like a Christmas tree. About forty-five messages across different mediums announced, 'Your first cruise has been cancelled.' It was because of this new COVID-19 virus. At this point, I'd vaguely heard about it, but no one back home had been worried.

Aboard a ship of 400 crew but no guests for a fortnight, we spent the first day sorting admin. Then we heard that our second two-week cruise had also been cancelled. Now, to my amazement, we'd have a month of waiting in Singapore. I was certain we'd get sent home, but they put us up in a hotel. We could access the ship at any time as long we had our temperature taken.

Like the rest of the world, we genuinely had no idea what was about to happen. So, for now, we boosted crew morale by hosting deck parties and barbeques. Then, the decision was made to keep *Ovation* in Singapore but move her to dry dock and relocate us to another hotel nearby.

A rumour circulated that we might start up again if everyone had a two-week quarantine. Getting ahead of the game, we began immediately. We took *Ovation* out to sea for a fortnight, bobbing about until we could then, hopefully, pick up guests from our next destination.

Little did we realise that we wouldn't touch dry land for 100 days.

During those first two weeks at sea, more cruises got cancelled. Then, the phrase 'pause of operations' was bandied about. If that happened, where would that leave us, stranded in the ocean? We just had to assume, at some point, that we'd resume cruising, and so followed our itinerary back up to the Mediterranean. At every port where we hoped to take on guests, the cruise got cancelled.

Finally, it seemed that our cruise from Dubai would go ahead. We even got as far as planning the 'layout meeting' (scheduling shipboard activities). Ten minutes beforehand, our Hotel Director, Kevin Huxham, asked if I was ready, to which I replied, 'Yes, but is this cruise going to happen?' Ten minutes later, an email arrived. It had been cancelled.

This was a massive turning point because 'crew change' had also been cancelled…meaning that everyone was stuck onboard indefinitely. The energy shifted. People began worrying about their jobs, finances, families, and whether they'd ever get home. We had forty-two nationalities on *Ovation, and* each of those forty-two nations now had different border regulations.

While we'd been sailing to different ports, even if we couldn't pick up guests, we'd been comforted by having a destination. But now, out at sea, we had no destination and no end in sight. If it hadn't been for the outstanding leadership of both Kevin and Captain Andrew Pedder, I'm not sure how we'd have coped. Having been quarantined on the ship for so long, our only consolation was being absolutely COVID-free.

We just had to keep ourselves entertained, and boy, we did everything imaginable. Any kind of skill or talent was shared: jujitsu classes, Cantonese classes, dance classes, music classes, swimming classes, quizzes, games, music, drum nights, karaoke, choir, needlepoint, poolside basketball. Every Friday, we had sports challenges. Anything to keep us occupied and stop us from going mad. My friend Bridget and I took everyone's temperature twice a day, every day, on their way to breakfast and lunch.

Nowhere let us dock to disembark, only to take on fuel and food (and this was just crew food; we never touched the guest food, kept in freezers downstairs in case we suddenly started up). Finally, Greece let us anchor off a small island near Piraeus. It had thirty-four wind turbines. I know because I counted them. There was nothing else to do.

Once every fortnight, we docked for fuel and supplies. Eventually, we asked the port agent for comfort goodies like chocolate, Pringles and Haribo. Our tuck shop in Guest Services became our only joy; the queue stretched back to the end of the ship. You've never seen so many people so desperate for a bag of peanuts; this little taste of home offered a sense of hope.

At last, there was a definite plan: the official 'pause of operations'. Seabourn had ships stranded all over the world.

Now, instead of flying people home, they decided to sail us. All our ships met in Gibraltar docked on the quayside in a military operation.

Each ship was assigned a different continent. With *Ovation* headed for Europe, I didn't need to disembark, but other nationalities had to join their designated ship. Once on board, there could be no cross-contamination. For instance, everyone leaving *Ovation* lived on Decks Eight and Nine of their new ship. They couldn't meet or interact with crew from other ships living on different decks. Therefore, each deck had its own mealtimes and recreational areas.

Finally, *Ovation* was en route to Amsterdam. Upon arrival, everyone had to wait for their flights. But as *Ovation* couldn't dock, transport from ship to land took 45 minutes on a bumpy old barge with no seats. You spent the entire ride clinging to a pole, everyone's suitcases suspended up high in a net. Meanwhile, *Ovation* became a 'hotel ship'. As Seabourn people gradually left, we took on European crew arriving from Carnival Corporation ships. They, in turn, stayed on *Ovation* until their flights came up.

By this time, it was May. I was doing cabin inspections with the staff captain when Bridget called: 'Your flight's just come in!' I began packing but didn't have a warm coat. When I'd left home in February, it had been for a summer contract on the other side of the world. I hadn't anticipated clinging to a pole on a bumpy old barge at 5 a.m. in Amsterdam. However, I'd recently been using a Seabourn black padded jacket. When I asked Kevin if I could take it with me, he said, 'Yes, just bring it back when we start up again.'

On May 27th, I touched down at Heathrow, where Dad picked me up. On our three-hour drive back to Nottingham, we saw three cars on the road.

Lockdown on Ovation, no guests, empty deck, empty pool, stunning sunset!

9. 'THIS COULD BE A HAPPY ENDING, PERFECT PLACE TO STOP THE SHOW'

Arriving home was a culture shock; I'd spent three months literally in a bubble. Throughout lockdown, I naively convinced myself that everything would be fine after Christmas. I had to believe this … because on land, I felt I had no purpose. Working at sea was my life, and it had been ripped away from me. Now, I couldn't even sing for my supper at the local pub. Like everywhere else, it was closed.

I got involved with charity events and kept active with online fitness classes led by my amazing trainer, Jay Alderton. I took walks to get in my 10,000 steps but had to change my route. I spent too much money buying coffee along the way.

Christmas came and went. New Year brought another lockdown. At my lowest ebb, I genuinely felt that ships would never come back. I'd left it too long to find a job on land; driven by anxiety, I applied online to pack boxes at Amazon. Honest work, but a far cry from my dream. However, when I reached the payment details page, I realised that with costs for the forty-minute journey, plus daily living expenses, I'd make less than £20 a week. I didn't submit the form. I continued my coffee-less walks and fitness programme with Jay and waited.

Then, in March, out of the blue, came a call from Live Business. They asked me to launch a new Saga ship in May. I remembered Mum's advice and asked, 'Can I get back to you?'

Two days later, Handré called. He asked me to relaunch *Ovation* in May.

I sat on these offers for two days, thinking everything through very carefully. My head said to go with Live Business; their entire office staff was like family. Yet, in my heart, I just didn't feel that my chapter had ended with Seabourn. By now, Seabourn was like family, too … but it wasn't just everyone in the office. It was the incredible teams on the ships. It was the guests.

I couldn't turn my back on that tidal wave of love and support. My heart was screaming Seabourn, and I've always followed my heart.

I flew out to join *Ovation* in Greece on 27th May 2021, twelve months to the day that I'd arrived home in Nottingham. I'd gone from my ultimate low to my ultimate high. I took with me that black padded Seabourn jacket and returned it to the ship. That was symbolic for me.

The moment I stepped on board, a nurse pinned me to the wall and shoved a swab up my nose. Then, it was two weeks in quarantine, but not without fun and games. Adorable Hotel Director Zoran Jacimovic had boobytrapped my suite with practical jokes: coffee in the showerhead, honey on the telephone, and an oversized teddy in my bed.

The overwhelming moment, which had me in tears, was, of course, welcoming back our guests. The first live song to be played on the ship was Queen's 'The Show Must Go On'. There was a feeling of excitement and buzz, especially as Greek authorities let us sail without masks; it felt like we were *really* back.

Prior to COVID, maybe once or twice a week, out on deck, I'd always had a 'pinch me' moment, thinking, *Is this really happening? Aren't I lucky?* Now, those moments happen two or three times a day.

I stayed on *Ovation* for the best part of the year – a deliberate move to help stability. Afterwards, Handré asked about my personal goals. I told him I'd like to do a World Cruise and launch a new ship, neither of which I'd ever done. He offered me the second half of a 2023 World Cruise on *Sojourn* from Bali to Barcelona. I was over the moon!

I arrived home from another contract on *Ovation* on 2nd December 2022, leaving three months to prepare for the World Cruise. On 17th December, I received a text from Handré: 'Have you got a minute for a call?' They wanted me to be Cruise Director for the *entire* World Cruise from the start of January to the end of May. Now, instead of having three months to prepare, I had less than three weeks!

I was very proud of everything achieved on that World Cruise. I'm also proud of everything I've managed to achieve before I turn 40. At the time of writing, my birthday is just one month away. I'm bringing together all the people I love for a huge celebration. Then I've been offered a 'Birthday Cruise' in October 2023 and another World Cruise in 2024. There's so much to look forward to!

If he'd known all this lay ahead, I'm not sure that Little Ross – changing into his PE kit in that alcove by the bin – would have believed it. But to Little Ross – and *all* the Little Ross' out there – I'd say don't ever change who you are. Don't ever listen to people telling you that you shouldn't be whatever and whoever you want to be.

Be you. And don't ever apologise for it.

Wear the feather boa.

Wear the sequined shoes.

Treat the world as your stage.

I'd also tell Little Ross to look out for mini roundabouts when he takes his second and third driving tests … and buy collectable *Star Wars* figures now because they're worth a fortune when you're older!

But I think the most important thing I'd tell Little Ross – which he doesn't realise at that age – is how important memories are whether you're either part of the memory or making it.

And I'd reassure him that Dad loves him just as much as Mum loves him.

At home, in lockdown helping with the local charities, in my Seabourn jacket...and bobble hat

Back at sea about to perform my first solo show back after the pause

EPILOGUE: 'YOU ARE WHAT YOU FEEL'

In late 2009, on the final night of an *Island Escape* cruise, I was putting up Christmas trees in the lounge before the new guests arrived the next day (for what turned out to be 'The Cruise From Hell'). Facing the doorway, I saw a lady pacing around outside as if she was looking for someone. Finally, she entered the lounge a bit flustered, grasping a black sequined scarf.

'Are you okay?' I asked, approaching her.

'I'm so glad I found you!' she replied. 'I had to find you! I had to find you!'

'Do you need some help?' I offered because normally, on a final night, when a guest needs to find someone, they want assistance with a suitcase or piece of lost property.

'No,' she went on. 'I need to tell you something, and I need to give you this.' She handed me the scarf.

'What is it?' I asked.

'My husband gave me this scarf,' she went on. 'We booked this cruise to come on holiday together. But he passed away. I didn't want to come on the cruise without him. But while he was in hospital, he went to the gift shop, bought this scarf, and then gave it to me and said, "That's for the cruise."'

This lady went on to explain that her friends eventually convinced her she should still take the holiday.

'When my husband passed away,' she told me, 'I thought I'd never laugh again. Or enjoy life again. And *you've* made me laugh again. So, I want you to have the scarf.'

Of course, I still have it because that moment reaffirmed that I was doing the right thing with my life.

People don't go on a cruise *just* to go on a cruise or just to go on holiday. It's used for something. To escape for a little, to breathe. Or for mental health. Maybe they've had a really bad year of physical health and just want to get away, and the doctor has said, 'Yes, you can go.' Perhaps something horrific has happened, which they need time and space to process.

Whatever it may be: if I can just, for a millisecond, help them forget everything on their shoulders; if I can offer that little golden moment they look back on in years to come; and if it makes them smile going through pictures on their iPad saying, 'Oh, look at that stupid outfit Ross wore when we crossed the Equator!'; then, for me, that's my life completely made.

It all goes back to my phrase, '*A day never ends if a memory is made.*'

In my job, making memories is *the* most important thing. Yes, there are other key elements to being a Cruise Director. Time management, creative scheduling. But for me, why do I do what I do? Well, a lot of people ask me that.

It's to make people smile, laugh and bring them joy because that's what brings *me* joy.

In the words of Sir Tim Rice …

> '… *if you think it, want it*

A DAY NEVER ENDS IF A MEMORY IS MADE

Dream it—then it's real
You are what you feel.

Thanks, Mum.

ACKNOWLEDGEMENTS: ' ... HOW CAN WE EVER SAY ALL THAT WE WANT TO ABOUT YOU?'

I couldn't turn 40 without acknowledging those special people who have changed and enriched my life.

My dad is the best: a superstar. Dad, I know I can be a pain at times, but I don't ever want you to forget that I will always love you endlessly. Thank you.

Grandma, you taught us to love unconditionally. You and Grandad gave Uncle David, Uncle Geoff and Mum support, empathy, and a loving home. That love has been passed down the generations. You are our Rose, always in bloom with a loving smile.

My newly married double-university graduate big brother Karl. Thanks for putting up with me all these years! Even though you hate musicals, you still watched all my school productions. As much as we disagreed as kids, you've always been there for me.

My nephews Oscar and Dominic, you have made me so proud through your school nativity, gymnastic competitions, archery classes, skate parks and ninja warriors. Now you're both performers as well! I love you both more than you could ever know or understand.

Our newest 'official' family additions: Kinga. I've never seen my brother as happy as you have made him. You have raised two incredible children, Michael and Livia, with whom I can't wait to share more adventures!

Uncle Geoff: hard-working, dedicated, and loving father to Leanne and Nadine. These two courageous, determined and utterly awesome mums raised my little rock stars Luke, Holly, Bo and Harriett.

Uncle David and Aunty Judy are my fellow travellers and adventurers. Thank you both for all that you are and all that you've done for me.

My godmother Sharon and her family: thank you for the effortless love and support! Melanie and Richard, I am honoured to be a godparent to Frankie, who brings me such joy. Congratulations, Melanie, on the expected arrival of Frankie's little sister. And Gareth, thanks for letting me be part of your family with Charlotte and Logan, from pitches to stages.

Thank you to Mr. Ward, my Toot Hill Comprehensive Music teacher, for his extra time invested in me. I still sing from the diaphragm, and when I'm holding a long note, I always remember to let it out slowly, as if I'm deflating a balloon.

My English teacher, Mrs Need: you helped me feel accepted. When you went away on holiday, you even gave me keys to look after your cats. Thank you for that great essay mark on how I'd design and stage *Much Ado About Nothing*. To this day, I'm convinced you engineered that coursework option just to help me out!

Emma, I've been so proud to have you in my life ever since 'Who Do You Think You Are?'. I love your entire family: Jacqui, Martin, Nick, Bec, Noa, Edan, Lauren and Cameron. Jacqui was the first person I'd ever met (outside my immediate family) who offered instant warmth, kindness, and generosity. Thank you all. You're not just friends – you're my family.

Sarah Hargreaves (née Aspinal): Thank you for being my Valentine, for those trips to the Moulin Rouge (kebab shop), and for sneaking away on A Level results day to join me in Nottingham's finest gay bar, NG1. We completely nailed that dance routine to Steps' 'One For Sorrow'.

Jill Coupe, thank you for our incredible friendship ever since Pontins. Thank goodness both our families decided to refurbish our chalets! I could not be a prouder godfather to Oliver.

Island Escape brought Daniella Beck into my life. To find such a real, authentic, and genuine friend is truly rare. With love also to Mummy and Daddy Beck.

For many years, I never thought I'd have gay male friends. That was before I met Alex Jones. Technically, on paper, we shouldn't get on. Warhammer models and computer games are light years from musicals, sequins, and sparkles. Yet it took no time at all for our friendship to cement. Thank you, Alex, for inviting me on that first night out to Manchester. You are a true gem ... and host the best themed parties.

During Lockdown, two special ladies entered my life. I am forever grateful for reconnecting with Louise, who saved me in more ways than she knows. Being Eva's godfather makes me so proud and happy. John and Veronica: Thanks for the love and support. Without you all, I wouldn't have reconnected with Gemma, Pippa, John and Melissa.

My second 'lockdown lady' is Elizabeth. Thanks for letting me be part of your Bingham community events, which I loved so much. You are an amazing lady doing so much for so many people.

Lorraine: You've brought such happiness and light not just to Dad but to us all. Thanks for letting us be part of your lovely family with Tabitha, Dom, Emmy, Henry, Amarni and Troy.

My IWOM Jayne: I adore you and everything you give to the world. And, of course, I couldn't forget Steve. Hilarious, cheeky, and a great cook. Oh, and I've heard he's alright with a golf club!

To my Seabourn family: Handré, your love, support and kindness are like no other. You are an utter gem in this world, and I am so incredibly honoured to call you a friend. You inspire me every day.

Marc and Graham, from day one, you have been genuine and utterly fabulous friends. Thank you for taking me under your wing and always making me feel welcome.

To the incredible Seabourn guests and crew: It has been the greatest honour of my life to be included in your vacations and contracts. I hope to have made you smile or helped create a memory. My love to you all.

To those no longer with me: Grandma and Grandad Roberts, thank you for the Christmases, the Sunday Roasts and ketchup on toast (it's amazing, dear reader; you should try it!).

Grandad Haynes: For the summer days in the vegetable patch and making wooden projects in the shed, through to cruising the Med, I thank you with all my heart.

To Paul Eastwood, a true superstar comedian, the laughs will last forever.

My godfather Karl: If I made the memories, you captured them. Thanks for all the love, support, and, of course, the photographs.

Aunty Anne, your smile, your heart, and your laugh are with me always.

And finally, thank you to Martin Milnes and StoryTerrace, without whom this adventure of writing my memoir would not have been possible. This amazing process has been a joy. It's been very emotional to see my life on the printed page, but Martin, your support and guidance have been invaluable.

I'd recommend StoryTerrace and their bookmaking process to everyone.

My Family (dad was taking the picture)

From performing Joseph in my childhood home front room with a homemade programme...

Oscar and Dominic

My Rock, My Dad

and then fulfilling and living my dream at my 40th Birthday Party and finally being Joseph, with confetti -obviously!

Turning the big Four Oh! In a sequin suit...naturally!

StoryTerrace

Printed in Great Britain
by Amazon

31202871R00076